the little
b...

B

Written and edited by Gill Knappett.
The author has asserted her moral rights.
Designed by Tim Noel-Johnson.
All photographs © Jarrold Publishing, except
pp16–17 (Thermae Bath Spa) and p38 (Jane Austen
Centre). The picture on the front cover (bl), pp69
and 86 is used by kind permission of the Bath
Postal Museum; the picture on p52 is used by kind
permission of The Jacob's Bakery Ltd. The quote
on p81 is reproduced by kind permission of
A. P. Watt Ltd on behalf of the Literary Executors
of the Estate of H. G. Wells.

Printed in Hong Kong.
ISBN 0-7117-2433-4                        1/03

Jarrold Publishing, Healey House, Dene Road, Andover,
Hampshire, SP10 2AA.
Tel: 01264 409200    e-mail: heritagesales@jarrold.com
website: www.britguides.com

## Introduction

From the early discovery of the bubbling hot springs so loved by the Romans, through its heady heyday as the fashionable social centre of Georgian life for flirting, flaunting, gossiping, gambling and 'taking the waters', today's visitor to Bath is in good company in this golden city renowned for its connections with the royal, the noble and the famous.

Delve into over 100 fascinating facts, figures and fables about Bath – one of Britain's most elegant cities, famed for its fine architecture – for an intriguing flavour of its splendid sights and secrets.

## Ancient waters

The hot springs of Bath originate from rain on the Mendip Hills being driven deep underground, to rise bubbling and hot to the surface. The water we see rising today fell as rain as long as 10,000 years ago.

## Springs have sprung

Three hot springs are located within the area of Bath's historic city centre: the Hetling and Cross Bath Springs in Hot Bath Street, and the principal spring – King's Spring – which rises within the site of the Roman Baths and Pump Room. These three mineral-rich springs provide the source of water for the city's newest spa complex – Thermae Bath Spa.

## Rising waters

In the King's Bath, the water rises at the rate of over one million litres (approximately 250,000 gallons) per day at a constant temperature of 46°C (115°F).

## Hot stuff

Bath's springs are the only hot springs in Britain.

## The legend of Prince Bladud

Legend has it that Bath was founded by Prince Bladud in 863 BC. Banished from his kingdom as a leper, he became a swineherd on the banks of the Avon. His pigs loved wallowing in the hot spring and Bladud noticed that as a result their skin sores disappeared, so he plunged himself into the mud and his leprosy was cured. When he became king he established his court at the place of the spring and built Caer Badon, the City of Bath.

## Acorny tale

Acorns carved into the stonework of many Georgian buildings in Bath reflect the legend of Prince Bladud and his pigs, who could only be enticed from the hot springs with their favourite food – acorns.

## The arrival of the Romans

The Romans built their sacred bathing
complex and the surrounding town c. AD 65.

## Sweating buckets

Visitors found that Bath's waters caused
them to perspire profusely – partly because
of the heat but also because of the 40
different minerals and elements it contains.

## Early central heating system

The Romans installed a sophisticated underfloor central heating system in the baths. Air was heated by a furnace and drawn by ducted flue beneath the rooms which were raised on brick *pilae*.

## Roman temple

The Romans built a temple dedicated to Sulis Minerva, the Celtic goddess of healing, within the complex of the grand spa. The bronze life-size head of the statue of Minerva from the Roman temple was discovered under Stall Street by workmen in 1727.

## Gorgon's head

The Gorgon's head in the Roman Baths, which once adorned the pediment of Bath's Roman temple, is not the female head with snakes for hair of conventional Roman mythology, but a fierce, wild-eyed male figure.

## Curses I

The Roman Baths display objects thrown into the sacred spring as offerings to the gods by the Romans; as well as coins and jewellery, there are curses scratched on rolled lead, including an inscription cursing a rival for the loss of a girlfriend.

## Curses II

The earliest recorded reference to the word 'Christian' in England is to be found

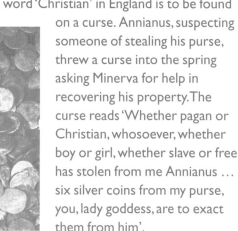

on a curse. Annianus, suspecting someone of stealing his purse, threw a curse into the spring asking Minerva for help in recovering his property. The curse reads 'Whether pagan or Christian, whosoever, whether boy or girl, whether slave or free has stolen from me Annianus … six silver coins from my purse, you, lady goddess, are to exact them from him'.

## Something old

Just as those today in search of the body beautiful invest in a variety of beauty treatments, the  Romans would sit in hot rooms and have dirt and hair scraped from the skin before sealing the pores by plunging into a cold bath. The bathing complex was also used as a place for exercise, with the Great Bath being a popular swimming pool.

## Something new

Thermae Bath Spa, opened in 2003, provides the only place in the UK for public bathing in natural thermal waters. The project, supported by a grant from the Millennium Commission, involved the restoration of five historic buildings – including the sacred Cross Bath – and the construction of a state-of-the-art building. Highlights include four bathing pools, including an open-air rooftop pool, a series of steam rooms, spa treatments and visitor centre.

## After the Romans

When the Romans left Britain in AD 410, the site of the baths regressed to its original marshy state. Six hundred years

later, to aid the infirm, Bishop John de Villula built the King's Bath over the Roman reservoir, using the same stone used by the Romans all those years previously.

## A spectator sport

In medieval times the King's Bath was used for mixed nude bathing and open to public view. Jeering spectators would sometimes throw animals – and each other – into the water.

## Sleazy reputation

Records show that in the 16th century five medieval baths were still in use, although sleazy and squalid in reputation.

## Unclean, unclean

In 1668, Samuel Pepys wrote of Bath and the bathing 'it cannot be clean to go so many bodies together in the same water'.

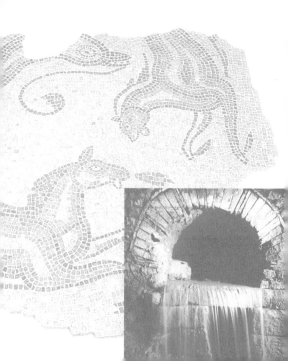

## Royal approval

During the early 1600s Queen Anne of Denmark, wife of James I, visited seeking a cure for dropsy, signalling the start of Bath's revival. A number of visiting royals led to the city's reconstruction as a fashionable resort in the 18th century.

## Great excavations

The great Roman Baths complex was rediscovered and excavated in the 1880s.

## Pile 'em high

Over the centuries, the baths were constructed on top of each other; 19th-century excavation revealed the extent of the Roman baths below ground level and the Queen's Bath, constructed next to the King's Bath during the 16th century, was removed in order to reveal the Roman baths below.

## Long lead lining

The Great Bath, hidden for centuries until being discovered in the 19th century, is 26-metres (85-feet) long and lined with 8.5 tonnes of Mendip lead.

## One mad …

In Georgian times, bathing took place in the early morning, with visitors to the baths arriving by sedan chair and being helped into voluminous bathing clothes before wallowing in warm water for up to an hour. Once the wet attire was removed, the bathers would return to their lodging houses wrapped in blankets and retire sweating to bed. Once cooled, it would be time to go out for a grand, public breakfast.

## … social …

After breakfast came the regular visit to the Pump Room to drink the recommended three glasses of mineral water and to meet for essential gossip. The rest of the morning would involve visits to coffee houses and reading rooms, and a service in the abbey. Post-lunch activities might include a promenade along the Parades – to see and be seen being the order of the day.

## ... whirl

After dinner, the evening's entertainment often included attending the theatre, gambling at a game of cards, and dancing in one of the assembly rooms. Bedtime was 11p.m. – for the sake of good health. It was a hard life!

## Towering infernos

In the 1770s the Assembly Rooms were frequented by the Macaronies, philandering fops who sported the latest bizarre hairstyles – at one time reaching heights of up to 150 centimetres (5 feet). To achieve such proportions, horsehair was mixed with lard and egg white and attached to a wire frame, with the wearer's own hair combed over the top. Such creations were known to catch fire when these fashion-conscious poseurs stood too close to candlelit chandeliers.

## Money well spent

A corporate syndicate financed the £20,000 venture to build the 18th-century Assembly Rooms as a social centre for late-Georgian Bath. When the Upper Assembly Rooms opened, 1,200 one-guinea (£1.05) tickets were sold, each giving entrance to one gentleman and two ladies; unaccompanied gentlemen could purchase half-guinea tickets.

## Changing rooms

Today the basement of the Assembly Rooms is home to the Museum of Costume, featuring regularly changing collections from the 16th century to the latest cutting-edge fashion designs.

## Water is best

The first Pump Room was opened in
1706 and rebuilt in the present style in
1791–5. A Greek motto inscribed under
its pediment in Stall Street proclaims
'Water is Best'.

## A cure for all

It was claimed that the waters had curative powers for many ailments including 'gout, rheumatism, palsies, convulsions, asthma, jaundice, the itch, scab, leprosy, scrofula, epilepsies, diseases of the eyes, deafness, noise in the ears, palpitations of the heart, sharpness of urine, wounds, ulcers, piles and infertility'.

## Queen mother

Mary, wife of James II, came to Bath in the hope that the effects of the waters would be a remedy for her infertility; she subsequently gave birth to a son.

## The first

Bath's Royal Mineral Water Hospital was the first in England to be open to rich and poor alike; a £3 deposit

on arrival paid for your transport home – or funeral, depending on the outcome of your confinement!

## Groaning wall

The dreadful moans of souls in pain have often been heard at the ancient Groaning Wall, next to the Mineral Water Hospital.

## Living in hope

Its wondrous cures have gained a world-
    wide fame,
Bath Mineral-Water Hospital is its name.
To all who feel an interest in my rhyme,
I'll tell now how the Inmates pass their
    time,
I can declare the truth of what I state,
To dwell amongst them it's now my fate.
For many months I lameness have
    endured
And by God's blessing hope to return
    home cured.

   From 'Lines Composed to Bath Mineral
                Water Hospital', c.1865

## Water to wine

To celebrate the coronation of Charles II in 1661, the mayor and corporation, preceded by 400 young virgins, drank the king's health from St Mary's Fountain which flowed with wine rather than water to mark the occasion.

## Motherly love

A visit to the city by Frederick, Prince of Wales, in 1738 was marked by the erection of an obelisk in Queen Square. His mother, Queen Caroline, reputedly disliked her son so much she said of him 'My dear first-born is the greatest ass, the greatest liar and the greatest beast in the whole world and I heartily wish he was out of it.'

## We are not amused

Royal Victoria Park is named after Princess Victoria who visited in 1830, before she became queen. Unfortunately the 11-year-old princess was bored during her visit and developed a lifelong hatred of the city. Many years later crowds gathered at the station to greet their sovereign on a scheduled visit during her journey from London to Bristol – but the train passed through the station with the queen's window blinds firmly shut!

## Diamond celebrations

The domed Victoria Art Gallery was opened to mark Queen Victoria's diamond jubilee and houses British and European art collections and contemporary art exhibitions.

## Jane Austen's home

No.4 Sydney Place was the home of Jane Austen and her family, who moved here in 1801 when her father retired as rector of Steventon in Hampshire. She lived here until 1804.

## Too dull for words

Though the heroines of Jane Austen's *Northanger Abbey* and *Persuasion* found love in the city, Jane herself found it a rather dull place, and the social constraints petty and tedious. She preferred to walk into the countryside and surrounding villages.

## The Jane Austen Centre

The Jane Austen Centre – situated in Gay Street where the author lived in 1805 – organizes walking tours of Jane Austen's Bath, starting from the KC Change visitor information centre and taking in the places where she lived, walked and shopped, as well as the settings which inspired her Bath-based novels – *Northanger Abbey* and *Persuasion*.

## The Blue Boy
Thomas Gainsborough (1727–88) painted his famous portrait, *The Blue Boy*, while staying at No.17 The Circus.

## Tears for Fears

Curt Smith and Roland Orzabal met as children in Bath and went on to form the successful pop duo Tears for Fears in the 1980s. Hits included 'Shout' and 'Everybody Wants to Rule the World'.

## Another planet

Musician and amateur astronomer William Herschel discovered the planet Uranus (originally called Georgium Sidus) from his Bath home at No.19 New King Street (now the William Herschel Museum) in 1781; he was later appointed court astronomer by George III.

## Charles Dickens

A young Charles Dickens first visited Bath in 1835 when he was a newspaper reporter. He stayed at The Saracen's Head in Broad Street, one of Bath's oldest pubs.

## Weller's wery warm water

In Dickens's *Pickwick Papers*, Mr Pickwick's faithful servant Sam Weller claimed Bath's spa waters to have 'a wery strong flavour o' warm flat irons'.

## The play's the thing

Richard Sheridan's famous comic plays *The Rivals* and *The School for Scandal* are set in Bath.

## General Wade's House

The National Trust Shop, with its fine Corinthian pilasters, is situated in Abbey Church Yard and was once home to General Wade – the MP for Bath and commander of the troops who built the military roads in Scotland to crush Jacobite resistance after the famous uprising of 1715.

## Caught on film

Lacock Abbey, near Bath, is where Fox Talbot conducted the first photographic experiments in the 1800s. It has also been the setting for several television and film productions, including *Pride and Prejudice* and *Harry Potter*.

## Queens' dowry

Corsham Court near Bath – now home to a collection of old masters dating from the 1500s – belonged to the Royal Family from Saxon to Elizabethan times, often forming part of the dowry of the queens of England in the late 14th and early 15th centuries.

## An admirable choice

Admiral Lord Nelson convalesced at
The Three Tuns (now called the Crystal
Palace) in Bath after being wounded at
the Battle of the Nile in 1798. He later
lived at No.88 Pierrepont Place with
his mistress, Lady Hamilton.

## Politically speaking

The 23-year-old Winston Churchill made his first political speech at Claverton Manor, near Bath, on 26 July 1897.

## American Museum

Since 1961 Claverton Manor has been home to the American Museum, the only museum in Europe illustrating domestic American life with its furniture, decorative arts and quilts dating from colonial times in the 17th century to the end of the 19th century.

## A Welsh influence

Welshman Richard 'Beau' Nash (1674–1762) was appointed Master of Ceremonies to impose order and civility. As the 'King Of Bath' he ruled for 50 years, transforming the status of the city by banning the wearing of swords, duelling and other anti-social behaviour, keeping the streets clean and welcoming wealthy visitors to keep the spa resort prosperous.

## Say cheese

When accused of being a whoremonger, Beau Nash is reputed to have said 'A man can no more be termed a whoremonger for having one whore, than a cheesemonger for having one cheese'.

## Popjoys

The buildings housing the Theatre Royal
and Garrick's Head pub were once the
home of Beau Nash. Popjoys restaurant
next door was home to his mistress Juliana
Popjoy, with whom he lived after a gambling
debt forced him to give up his home.

## A hollow ending

When Beau Nash died his mistress Juliana Popjoy vowed never to sleep in another man's bed – and, legend has it, spent the last years of her life in the hollow of an old oak tree!

This was the splendid home of Beau Nash, "The King of Bath," and his handsome and faithful mistress Juliana Popjoy. They spent the whole of the latter part of their lives here – until the Beau's death, in 1761, at the age of 86.

We preserve in this building all the high standards Beau Nash set for Bath. We think that Juliana Popjoy approves. Indeed, she is occasionally seen here, dressed in grey, and we suspect she has an eye on whether we are entertaining our guests as well as she entertained the Beau's friends in the same rooms 250 years...

## Bath Oliver

The Bath Oliver is an unsweetened biscuit invented in the 1700s by Dr William Oliver, co-founder of the Royal Mineral Water Hospital in Bath, as part of a diet for his overweight patients. On his deathbed Dr Oliver bequeathed the secret recipe for Bath Olivers to his faithful coachman John Atkins, who went on to make his fortune manufacturing the biscuits from his shop in Green Street.

## Bath chair

The Bath chair – a three-wheeled conveyance for invalids – was a familiar sight on the streets in the 19th century. Invented by local man Arthur Dawson, it could be pulled or pushed by just one man, ousting the sedan chair which required two men to carry it.

## Bath bun

The Bath bun is a spiced currant bun with a sugary topping – not to be confused with the Sally Lunn bun, also baked in Bath.

## Sally Lunn's buns

Sally Lunn, a Huguenot refugee, came to work at a bakery in Bath in 1680, bringing her recipe for brioche with her. Her buns were so popular that the bakery became a fashionable meeting place and the buns took on her name, although some say that Sally Lunn is rhyming slang for 'bun', and others think it derives from the French 'sol et lune' (sun and moon) which describes the colour and shape of the cake before and after it is cut.

## Oldest Bath house

Sally Lunn's House in North Parade
Passage claims to be the oldest house in
Bath, despite its 17th-century appearance.
Excavations in the cellar have shown

remains of Roman,
Saxon and medieval
buildings on the
site. The house is
now a restaurant
and museum, where
Sally Lunn buns are
still baked and her
kitchen and faggot
oven can be viewed.

## First king of England

The coronation of Edgar, the first ruler of all England, took place in the abbey church on Whit Sunday 973; all coronations since have been modelled on the original ceremony.

## A flourishing trade

At one time Bath had an important wool trade. In the 13th century, the monks residing at Bath Monastery, owned by the priory – now the site of the abbey – made their living from wool and cloth making.

## The Wife of Bath

Chaucer immortalized Bath as the centre of the cloth trade in the west of England in 'The Wife of Bath's Tale' from his *Canterbury Tales*.

## What a whopper

After the Norman Conquest, John of Tours – Bishop of Bath – built a church worthy of its new status as a cathedral. It was so big that the present church could have been contained in its nave. Today's structure dates from 1499 and was one of the last great churches to be built before the Reformation.

## An abbey by any other name ...

Bath Abbey is an abbey in name only, since the Dissolution of the Monasteries brought the role of the abbey to an end in the 1530s.

## Sweet dreams

A dream inspired Bishop Oliver King to rebuild the abbey in 1499. He dreamt he saw angels ascending and descending a ladder between heaven and earth, and heard a voice saying 'Let an Olive establish the Crown and a King restore the Church'. Oliver King took the words to represent his name and set about rebuilding the abbey. Carvings either side of the west front depict his vision.

## Never a truer word

The Latin inscription across the great west door of Bath Abbey fittingly reads 'Behold, how good and pleasing it is'.

## By royal order

Shocked by the unfinished state of the abbey on a visit to Bath in the 16th century, Elizabeth I ordered collections to be made throughout the land for seven years to fund building work.

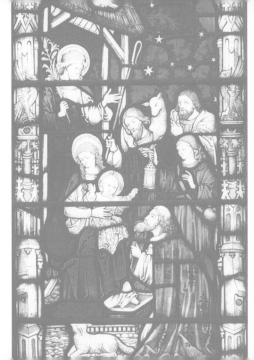

## The Lantern of the West

Bath Abbey is known as 'The Lantern of the West' because of the effect of its 52 windows, which occupy 80 per cent of the wall space, flooding the interior with light.

## Recycled glass

Pieces of the original shattered glass from Bath Abbey's east window – damaged by a landmine explosion in 1942 – can be seen in Toronto Cathedral, taken there with fragments from other British churches by a Canadian soldier who served here during the war.

## Tindall's testimony

The statue of the Risen Christ, by local sculptor Laurence Tindall, situated outside the abbey, depicts Christ rending the funeral clothes that bind his body, rather than the more usual image of him emerging from the tomb.

## Did you know …?

In the 18th century, a city fire engine was kept in the space below the organ in the north transept of the abbey.

## That's entertainment

The Abbey Church Yard was described more than 300 years ago by Daniel Defoe as a place of 'raffling, gaming and levity'; today it is often frequented by street entertainers including musicians and jugglers.

TRIM STREET

## What's in a name?

'Of all the towns in the kingdom Bath is
the most extraordinary, not to say
ridiculous, in its topographical and street
nomenclature … it is slightly bewildering
to find one of its narrowest streets 'Broad
Street', its 'North Road' leading due south
… Trim-street is not particularly trim,
Cheap-street is not particularly cheap,
nor is Green-street *very* green …'

M.J.B. Baddeley,
*Bath and Bristol and Forty Miles Around*, 1902

# The Bath house

A typical Bath house is a combination of a Bath stone façade, Welsh slate roof and wooden doors and sash windows, with a wide sandstone pavement outside.

## Out like a light

Iron cones known as link snuffers can still be seen beside several front doors in Bath, survivors of an era when burning torches were used to guide people through the dark streets at night and extinguished when they reached home.

## Eighteenth-century entrepreneur

Ralph Allen (1693–1764), known as the 'Man of Bath', was an influential figure in the city's golden age. He made his fortune from his reformation of Britain's inland postal service, and from his investments in the oolitic limestone quarries of Combe Down, which provided the stone from which much of the city is built.

## Classically Roman

The innovative designs of John Wood the Elder (1704–54) resulted in the spectacular architecture seen in Bath today. His interpretation of Bath as a new Roman city with a circus, forum and squares was strongly influenced by Palladio's use of the classical style.

## Fancy that

The Circus is said to resemble the Colosseum of Rome turned inside out and its diameter matches that of Stonehenge.

## Can't see the Wood

In the late 18th century, The Circus – designed by John Wood the Elder – had plane trees planted in its centre which, when fully grown, are reputed to have given rise to the saying 'can't see the Wood for the trees'.

## Mysterious symbols

The ornate frieze running
along the top of the
Doric columns at ground
floor level in The Circus
is decorated with stone

carvings. There are many theories
concerning the meaning of the carvings:
some say they represent the arts, the
sciences and occupations; others believe
them to be taken from a 17th-century
fortune-telling book; and some consider
them to be Masonic symbols. Did John
Wood leave a coded message in
the metopes?

## Like father, like son

John Wood died in 1754 when construction of his greatest masterpiece, The Circus, had barely begun, leaving his son to complete the work. John Wood the Younger went on to create the magnificent Royal Crescent. Between them, father and son left a legacy of more than 200 buildings in Bath.

## Europe's finest

Royal Crescent, designed to enfold Bath's open landscape, was built between 1767 and 1774. The 200-metre (650-foot) crescent was Britain's first and is still regarded as the finest in all of Europe.

## It's no joke

Royal Crescent is separated from the park below by a ha-ha – a cleverly constructed wall, invisible from the street above, originally built to prevent grazing animals from straying onto the crescent.

## Digging for victory

During the Second World War, the park in front of Royal Crescent was dug up and became allotments for growing vegetables.

## The Grand Old Duke of York

No. 1 Royal Crescent, home to the Duke of York in 1796, is today owned by the Bath Preservation Trust. Now a museum, it has been restored and furnished in authentic Georgian style.

## Sur le pont

Pulteney Bridge is the only bridge in England lined with shops on both sides. It was designed by Robert Adam, who was the winner of a young architect's competition, and completed in 1770, allowing the city to expand to the other side of the river.

## Italian comparison

'Miss Grammont was moved to declare the Pulteney Bridge with its noble arch, its effect of height over the swirling river, and the cluster of houses above, more beautiful than the Ponte Vecchio at Florence.'

H.G. Wells, *The Secret Places of the Heart*, 1933

## Widest street

Great Pulteney Street is the widest in Bath, the buildings either side standing 30 metres (100 feet) apart.

## Taxi rank

Two elegant pavilions in Queen's Parade Place were built for sedan chair runners waiting for trade, in an attempt to keep them away from the inns and alcohol that made them rude to their clients. This effort to introduce regulation was a forerunner of Hackney Carriage licensing.

## City vineyard

During the early part of the 18th century, The Vineyards in Bath covered 2.5 hectares (6 acres) and were noted for their muscadine grapes. A run of poor crops caused the vineyard to close around 1730.

## Off centre

Just as the building of the graceful sweep
that is Camden Crescent was nearing
completion, a landslip caused five of the
houses to collapse. As a result the terrace
was never finished, which is why the
pediment is not central.

## Eccentric's edifice

Just 2.4 kilometres (1.5 miles) from the city centre is Beckford's Tower, a monument commissioned by the eccentric author, traveller, scholar and collector William Beckford. Climbing the 156 steps to the top offers panoramic views of the surrounding countryside.

## Mr Bowler's Business

A family firm in business for 97 years is reconstructed in the Museum of Bath at Work. As well as being engineers, brass founders, gas-fitters, bell-hangers and locksmiths, the industrious J.B. Bowler & Sons also manufactured fizzy drinks and repaired soda-water machinery.

## First post

On 2 May 1840 the world's first letter with a postage stamp was sent from Bath Post Office at No.8 Broad Street, now home to the Bath Postal Museum.

## Bargain hunt

Bath is recognized as one of the most important centres outside London for antiques. Browse for treasures in Bartlett Street Antique Centre, Paragon Antique Market or, on Saturdays, Walcot Street – host to a flea market on the site of the old cattle market.

## Mozartfest

The Mozartfest provides an annual autumn celebration of Mozart's music, held in Bath Abbey and the 18th-century settings of the Assembly Rooms and Guildhall.

## Spring celebration

The Bath International Music Festival is held in late May and early June each year. The event is traditionally heralded with a free opening night celebration in Royal Victoria Park with fireworks, music and a hot-air balloon fiesta.

## Touché

The Dell in Royal Victoria Park was once a wild and remote spot where men would settle their differences with a duel. It is possible that some who met their fate here still visit, because early-morning strollers have heard the clash of steel, accompanied by a sudden and mysterious chill in the air …

## Let me out of here!

Jane Austen frequented Sydney Gardens, the oldest park in Bath and in her time a labyrinth so complicated that maps of its layout were sold. Concerts were often held here, and Jane reported that she was glad 'that the gardens are large enough for me to get pretty well beyond the reach of its sound'.

## Holburne Museum

The Sydney Hotel, at the heart of Sydney Gardens, was transformed into the Holburne Museum in 1916 and is home to Sir William Holburne's art collection formed in 19th century Bath, as well as providing a venue for major exhibitions.

## Lancelot's legacy

Prior Park, owned by The National Trust, provides a fine example of a garden landscaped by Lancelot 'Capability' Brown. Brown gained his nickname from his proud claim to find 'great capability of improvement' in any park or garden.

## Sporting life

Bath is renowned
for its sporting
links, particularly
highlighted by a
first-class rugby
union side,
annual cricket
festival, a national
sporting centre
of excellence at
the University,

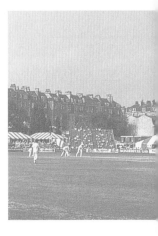

and an unusual kidney-shaped racecourse
on Lansdown Hill, with fantastic views
overlooking the city.

## World famous

The city of Bath was designated a World
Heritage Site in 1987.

## The finest place on earth

'Bath is the finest place on earth, for you may enjoy its society and its walks without effort or fatigue.'

James Boswell (1740–95)